BRITAIN'S 🏰 HERITAGE

Dinky Toys

David Busfield

AMBERLEY

Acknowledgements

A book of this nature is just not possible without the help of others and I would like to thank the following people: Sheila Golden for allowing me to use information provided to me by the late Peter Golden; David Dawson for the loan of models, proof reading the text and offering invaluable suggestions; and finally my partner Julie for proof reading and her patience while I spent a significant amount of time at the computer and taking the photographs. The photograph on p. 6 is reproduced courtesy of National Museums Liverpool.

First published 2017

Amberley Publishing
The Hill, Stroud
Gloucestershire, GL5 4EP

www.amberley-books.com

Copyright © David Busfield, 2017

The right of David Busfield to be identified as the Author of this work has been asserted in accordance with the Copyrights, Designs and Patents Act 1988.

ISBN 978 1 4456 6580 1 (paperback)
ISBN 978 1 4456 6581 8 (ebook)

British Library Cataloguing in Publication Data.
A catalogue record for this book is available from the British Library.

Printed in the UK.

Contents

1
Introduction

In 1931 Meccano Ltd introduced a range of diecast toys that were originally called 'Modelled Miniatures', and these were an instant success. The name was changed to 'Dinky Toys' in 1934 and the range was significantly increased in size. By the late 1930s they were popular with children throughout the world, while the word 'Dinky' became synonymous with many similar toys from different manufacturers.

Due to their high quality, this incredible success continued after the war until, in the 1950s, serious competition arrived from the likes of Corgi Toys, Matchbox and other makes. To this day Dinky Toys are still prized possessions by collectors in every corner of the world. Dinky remains a name to conjure with, and miniature vehicles bearing the name can still be bought new today. However, this book confines itself to the toys made in England by the original Meccano company, with a particular focus on the 'golden age', encompassing toys made between the end of the Second World War and the early 1960s, which brought such joy to so many – the era when Dinky toys were what every boy wanted.

The young boy in the 1950s could totally lose himself in a wonderful make-believe world where he could drive a car, a truck, a military tank or a bus, or be a policeman directing traffic. Similarly he could fly an aeroplane or sail a ship on the seven seas. The only limiting factor in this wondrous world was his imagination. He could race his blue-and-yellow Ferrari against other similar racing cars in the school playground with his friends.

At Christmas time he would see the correctly sized oblong present under the tree and open it with some considerable apprehension – would it be the missile system? ... Would it be the missile system? ... Yes! – it was a Corporal missile and his dreams had all come true.

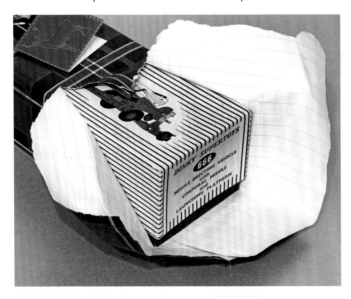

Christmas dreams.

2

Frank Hornby and Meccano

Frank Hornby was born in Copperas Hill, Liverpool, on 15 May 1863, and married Clara Walker Godefoy in 1887. Frank had two sons, Roland and Douglas, and a daughter, Patricia. His hobby was sheet-metal working and he devised a system using metal strips with regularly spaced holes that could be bolted together to produce models. He initially made this for his two sons, but then realised that there was a possibility of selling the system commercially. He took out his first patent in 1901. This was called 'Mechanics Made Easy' and was later in 1907 to be renamed Meccano. Over the next few years, this became a hugely popular construction toy for children. Frank Hornby died on 21 September 1936. During his lifetime he had created one of the greatest toy empires of all time. Meccano Ltd was hugely successful all over the world.

Frank Hornby, the founder of the Meccano empire.

Did you know?

The founder of Meccano, Frank Hornby was elected as the Conservative MP for the Everton district of Liverpool in 1931. Unfortunately at that time he was already suffering from ill-health, primarily diabetes. He chose not to stand for re-election in 1935.

The Binns Road factory in Liverpool opened in 1914, and by 1963 it employed 2,000 people, 80 per cent of them being women. From this factory came a number of famous brands: Meccano, Hornby Trains, Hornby Dublo, Dinky Toys, Dinky Builder and the *Meccano Magazine*. Bayco came under the Meccano umbrella, but it was a product they acquired when they took over the Plimpton Engineering Co. in 1959. At its height Meccano had factories in Binns Road, Liverpool, Speke and Aintree, plus manufacturing facilities in Argentina, France, Germany, the US and Spain. Meccano Ltd was the largest toy manufacturer in Britain during the 1920s and 1930s, and all products made by Meccano are still very popular with collectors today. A number of thriving clubs, covering the different types of products, cater for the many enthusiasts worldwide.

One of the production lines at Meccano Ltd, Liverpool, in 1932. The moving belt contains Dinky animals and figures being painted and also Hornby '0' gauge petrol tankers. (Courtesy of National Museums Liverpool: Stewart Bale collection, Merseyside Maritime Museum)

After the death of Frank Hornby in 1936, Meccano was taken over by his son Roland Hornby. With the advent of the Second World War, things began to get difficult as steel prices started to rise; eventually all toy manufacturing stopped and the factory was turned over to war production.

After the war Meccano returned to its core business and the good times returned for a short period. Due to a succession of problems – including industrial disputes, a lack of investment in machinery, old-fashioned working practices, increased competition, management complacency and the changing desires of children – Meccano went into a period of serious decline. In 1964 Meccano was taken over by Lines Brothers, the makers of Tri-ang. They had at one time been one of the largest toymakers in the world, but they were unable stop the serious problems and, in 1971, all of the Lines Group went into liquidation. The Meccano name was then reinstated and sold to the Airfix Group. Sadly, things did not improve and the Binns Road factory finally closed on 30 September 1979. This did not save Airfix, and they later called in the receiver. At the time of writing, Airfix was part of Hornby Hobbies and the Dinky Toys brand was owned by Mattel Inc.

A selection of Meccano products with Dinky Toys, Hornby Railways, Hornby Dublo and Meccano. The Ferris wheel is a factory-built item supplied to dealers.

3
1931–1939: The Birth of Dinky Toys

By the early 1930s Hornby O gauge trains had become a stunning success story, and in 1931 Meccano launched a totally new range of diecast toys in the marketplace with two items: the No. 1 Station Staff gift set and the iconic No. 13 Hall's Distemper Advertisement. These were initially called 'Hornby Series Modelled Miniatures' and were promoted as items to 'Add Realism to Your Railway'.

Over the next three years, the range grew significantly and, in April 1934, the name was changed to Meccano Dinky Toys and then shortened to just Dinky Toys. The name 'Dinky Toys' was the idea of George Jones, who was the sales director at Meccano; he also came up with the 'Dublo' name.

By 1934 there were seventy-eight diecast toys in the range. These included cars, commercial vehicles, trains, figures, animals, a military tank and the distemper advertisement. With the exception of the Hall's advert, all the other items were available individually or as a gift set. The first vehicles were mostly generic models and not based on real-world vehicles. The only named item was the No. 22e, identified as a Fordson Tractor in the December 1933 *Meccano Magazine*.

Meccano were not the first in the diecast field. TootsieToy in the US were already making vehicles and companies such as Britains and Johillco were manufacturing figures in the UK. By the mid-1930s, Dinky Toys were selling very well in their own right and the brand quickly became a household name for diecast models.

An example of the variation in branding is shown on p. 9 with two different labels, but the same box contents.

The first advertisement for Dinky Toys in the April 1934 *Meccano Magazine*. The rarest item on here now is the 'Hall's Distemper Advertisement'; the figures are diecast but the advertisement is cardboard.

Two pre-war sets showing the Hornby Modelled Miniatures branding and then the change to Dinky Toys. Both sets contain the same figures.

Did you know?

The *Meccano Magazine* was published by Meccano Ltd from 1916 to 1963. It was unique in the British toy industry for a company to have such an influential in-house magazine. It was a general hobby magazine intended for 'boys of all ages'. It was free at first but a charge was levied from 1918 onwards. Originally intended for Meccano builders, its scope was widened to include engineering, trains, aircraft, motor vehicles and many other topics. The *Meccano Magazine* continued with other publishers from 1963 until 1981, when it ceased altogether. Copies of the *Meccano Magazine* are excellent reference documents.

The very first items were made from lead but this was quickly changed to mazac, which is a zinc alloy comprising 3–4 per cent aluminium, 1–2 per cent copper and 92–96 per cent zinc. These materials have to be absolutely pure, otherwise intercrystalline corrosion (sometimes erroneously called fatigue) will occur. Unfortunately, many of the pre-war and some of the post-war Dinky Toys suffered from this problem, and sadly this did not just affect Dinky but also a lot of other manufacturers as well. An extreme example of intercrystalline corrosion can clearly be seen in the 52a Queen Mary Liner. Some post-war Dinky Toys are made from aluminium.

The severe effects of intercrystalline corrosion, sometimes incorrectly referred to as 'fatigue' on the *Queen Mary*. She is not very seaworthy now.

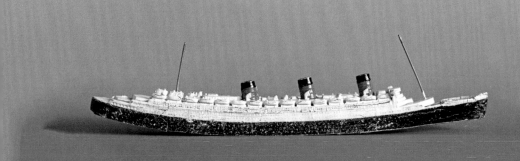

The range of figures produced by Meccano was very comprehensive and included passengers, station staff, railway engineering staff and railway attendants. While these sets were sold both before and after the war, there are differences. The pre-war models were slightly larger and the level of detail in the painting was greater than in the post-war figures. Note the porter carrying a suitcase with the initials 'FH', for 'Frank Hornby'.

In July 1936 Meccano introduced the 'Dolly Varden' Doll's House, which was to a scale of approximately 1:20 (a specific scale was never mentioned in any of the Meccano literature). The house was made of reinforced leather board. There were four sets of Dinky Toys furniture available for the house, which featured dining room, bedroom, kitchen and bathroom settings. The 'Dolly Varden' range never reappeared after the war, and is now the rarest of all Dinky Toys to find. This is not surprising, as they were made from board and will now be seventy years old. The name 'Dolly Varden' appears on the front door of the house; she was the daughter of a London locksmith in *Barnaby Rudge* by Charles Dickens.

Pre-war figures showing the high level of painting detail, especially on the faces. The post-war figures were slightly smaller than these.

The 'Dolly Varden' Doll's House with four sets of furniture. Because the house is made of board and not wood, not many have survived and they are now very rare.

As the pre-war range gained momentum, a lot of the models were now named after the vehicle they represented and were very faithful to actual real-world vehicles. In October 1934 Meccano advertised '150 Varieties'; by August 1935 it was 200; by February 1937 it was 250; and by April 1938 it was 300. The range, immediately before the Second World War, was very varied, encompassing motor cars, commercial vehicles, buses, aeroplanes, military vehicles, motorcycles, miniature trains, railway accessories, figures, animals, street furniture, buildings and a pavement set. This breadth of range was not seen after the war.

The 162a Light Dragon Tractor, which is shown with the seated soldiers, is fitted with rubber wheels. This was because of a shortage of metal at the start of the war.

With the advent of the Second World War, toy production slowed significantly due to the difficulty of obtaining raw materials and, in September 1943, the Meccano Factory was turned over totally to war production. The major item to come out of Binns Road during the war was a bomb release mechanism used on the RAF bombers, although they did manufacture a lot of other items. After the war, priority was given to the production of Dinky Toys over Hornby Dublo. However, as the factory had to have significant changes in order to get back to the traditional product ranges, it was to be some considerable time before Dinky Toys would once again be readily available.

Right: Pre-war vehicles and motorcycles. The tractor was among the very first Dinky vehicles to be made in 1933.
Below: Pre-war trains, boats and planes. The streamlined train set, based on the LNER's Silver Jubilee, was made in numerous colour schemes. It was reissued after the war in British Railway colours.

4
1948–1953 : Start of a New Era

In the spring of 1945, the government-imposed war work was beginning to slow down and Meccano were starting to look at how they could redevelop their traditional business. Due to severe paper shortages during the war, the *Meccano Magazine* was reduced in size from its old A4 format to a smaller A5 version, together with a significant reduction in the number of pages. From June 1945 promises of toys becoming available again were repeatedly made, but their appearance in the UK was delayed by the governmental imposition of 'Export or Die', which was forced upon manufacturers in order to reduce the significant war debt, owed primarily to America.

The first positive signs of news about Dinky Toys came in April 1946, when 'New Dinky Toys Now Ready' was announced in the magazine. These were the 38c Lagonda Sports Coupe, a reissue of a pre-war car and the 153a Military Jeep, the latter being the first of the new post-war castings. Due to the export drive, there were very limited numbers of these two models in the home market for some considerable time.

Above left: The first post-war advertisement for Dinky Toys in the *Meccano Magazine*: the 153a Jeep was the first all-new casting. Other items were reissues of pre-war vehicles.
Below: The Dinky Toys Jeep: the version on the left with the solid steering wheel is the earliest. The later version on the right has a domed bonnet.

Did you know?

Dinky Toys are fun to collect and some of them command a very high price due to their rarity. However, as in many collecting areas, there are dubious practices. Repainted Dinky Toys are worth a fraction compared to a genuine original, but some of these repaints are done to a very high standard. Honest sellers will always describe items appropriately but some do not. *Caveat emptor*, or buyer beware.

The December 1946 *Meccano Magazine* was much more confident of stock availability in toy shops and the range had now grown, although still included a mix of re-released pre-war and new post-war castings. At this time Dinky Toys were issued to dealers in trade boxes that usually contained either three, four or six models. When purchasing an item one model would have been taken from the trade box and given to the customer; if the toy was the last in the box the packaging would have been thrown away by the dealer or offered to the customer. A limited number of original trade boxes are still in existence today but some of these are very rare.

All small Dinky Toys models were supplied to dealers in trade boxes up until 1953, when individual boxes were introduced.

One of the most significant announcements was made in October 1947, when Meccano advertised the introduction of Dinky Supertoys. This was a range of Foden DG diesel-powered eight-wheel trucks, a range of Guy 4-ton trucks and the Shetland Flying Boat. These models represented a significant new direction for Dinky Toys, as they were much larger than all the previous diecast models in the range. They must have appeared on lots of Christmas-present lists in 1947. In his book *History of British Dinky Toys*, Cecil Gibson erroneously stated that the Dinky Guy was an Otter. This model was, in fact, based on a Vixen. The Guy Otter was a 5–6 ton vehicle, while the Vixen was Guy's 4-ton vehicle.

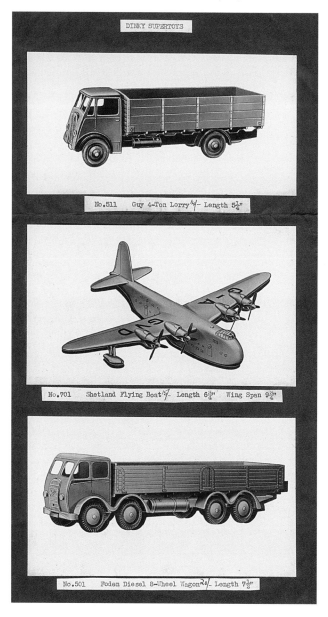

An original Meccano half-tone publicity image of the first Dinky Supertoys from 1948.

Dinky Supertoy Foden trucks showing the early Type 1 and the later Type 2 cabs.

All Dinky commercial vehicles look very purposeful when carrying loads. The barrels and crates on the electric vehicle are from the French Dinky range.

The first Dinky Foden castings were based on the DG vehicle, but these were superseded in 1952 by the more modern Foden FG cab; these are referred to as 'Type 1' or 'Type 2' cabs. Many collectors believe that these models were the finest vehicles produced by Dinky and, looking at how faithful they are to the real-world vehicle, this is understandable. They are still highly sought after today.

Dinky commercial vehicles look very purposeful when fitted with loads. In the real world, these trucks were rarely seen empty. Did Dinky miss an opportunity here to produce some accessories that would have added to the play value?

Dinky Toys always had an excellent offering of construction models and the three imposing Dinky Supertoys are no exception. The 561 Blaw Knox Bulldozer had an ingenious mechanism whereby a lever could be operated alongside the driver to raise, or lower, the front blade. The 562 Muir Hill Dump Truck had the driver sitting on a seat that could be rotated 180 degrees and also had a tipping bucket, just like the real vehicle. The 563 Blaw

Knox Heavy Tractor was effectively the bulldozer but without the blade. All three vehicles were fitted with a tow hook.

When a new Dinky Toy was being produced, a small batch of castings would be painted in a number of different colour schemes; these would be presented to the Meccano new product committee and the sales director for their perusal. All these samples would have a tie-on tag attached to them, showing exactly what shades of paint had been used on them. One, or possibly two, of these samples would then be selected as the versions that were to go into production, while the other unwanted samples would then be discarded. These paint samples are incredibly rare items, and I have only been able to find documentary evidence of fifteen surviving examples. There must be more and hopefully they will turn up sometime.

The same process would be repeated when sales started to slow down on existing models in the range. New colour schemes would be introduced to replace the old ones. A good example of colour schemes is shown, with eight different variations of the 34b Loudspeaker Van.

Left: Construction vehicles from Blaw-Knox and Muir-Hill.
Below: A Daimler Saloon factory paint sample with its original approval label.

Right: Four factory paint samples: the bus colour scheme was not approved, which is why that label has not been signed.
Below: The 34b Loudspeaker Van, showing eight different colour variations for the same model.

Meccano was noted for the fine quality of its marketing publicity and the Dinky Toys catalogues upheld that tradition. The October 1953 catalogue listed details of 114 models, illustrated in full colour and priced. It can clearly be seen here that the breadth and scope of the Dinky range never matched the numbers seen before the war. Other variations of this catalogue were available for overseas markets and these were translated as appropriate.

There was also a regular supply of information for dealers in regards to forthcoming models with regularly updated order forms and other important documentation.

May 1947 saw the launch of the original car in the iconic 40 series of vehicles, which was the 40a Riley Saloon. The other cars were the 40b Triumph 1800 Saloon, the 40e Standard Vanguard Saloon, the 40d Austin Devon Saloon, the 40g Morris Oxford Saloon, the 40f Hillman Minx Saloon, the 40j Austin Somerset Saloon and the 40h Austin Taxi. These were popular vehicles seen every day on British roads, and this became one of the most successful ranges for Meccano.

The front cover of the 1953 Dinky Toys catalogue. All Meccano publicity material was of the highest quality.

A flier dated January 1953 that was sent out to dealers, showing new model introductions. The crane was marketed as a Dinky Toy but made to '0' gauge scale and was suitable for the Hornby railway system.

The 40e Standard Vanguard had two distinct casting variations: the first version from 1948 has open rear wheel arches, which were then changed to covered wheel arches to reflect the real-world vehicle more realistically.

Also at this time another very important range of commercial vehicles was the 25 series, with many of these now regarded as classic Dinky Toys. This range started in 1948 with the

Examples of the 40 series Dinky Toys cars – an extremely important range in the early 1950s.

The 40e Standard Vanguard Saloon: on the left is the early version with open rear wheel arches. The later version is on the right.

25p Aveling Barford Diesel Roller, the 25m Bedford End Tipper, the 25r Forward Control Lorry, the 25g Small Trailer, the 25w Bedford Truck and the 25x Commer Breakdown Lorry. These were a charming range of commercial vehicles, some with excellent working features. The Forward Control Lorry was based on a Leyland Beaver.

The very popular farm and garden range of products commenced in 1948. These items were as follows: 27a Massey-Harris Farm Tractor, the 27b Halesowen Harvest Trailer, the 27c Massey-Harris Manure Spreader, the 27g Motocart, the 27f Estate Car, the 27h Disc Harrow, the 27f Land Rover, the 27m Land Rover Trailer, the 27k Hay Rake and the 27n Field-Marshall Tractor. This delightful range of farm vehicles was very comprehensive and provided huge amounts of play value. The unidentified Motocart was made by Opperman and the Estate Car was made by the American company Plymouth. The milk churns shown on the Motocart are Hornby accessories.

Dinky Toys always had an excellent range of emergency vehicles, and this period was no exception. Between 1948 and 1953 two vehicles were pre-war reissues and three vehicles were new castings. The reissued vehicles were the 25h Streamlined Fire Engine and the

The 25 series commercial vehicles. The 25v Refuse Wagon was in the catalogue from 1948 to 1965; the final version was fitted with windows.

The 1950s Farm and Garden range. The Massey Harris Tractor was in the range for eighteen years and was fitted with more realistic rubber tyres in its final form.

30f Ambulance, while the new vehicles were the 30h Daimler Ambulance, the 555 Fire Engine with Extending Ladder and the 30hm Daimler Ambulance.

The two pre-war vehicles were generic rather than being based on real-world vehicles, although there has been much conjecture on their identity. The post-war Fire Engine was based on a Commer chassis.

The strange anomaly is that, during this period, the Dinky range did not include a police car. The 30hm Daimler Ambulance was an export-only item for the US market, which was a strange choice as the real-world Daimler Ambulance was never used by any military forces.

The 23 series range of racing cars was made up of reissues and new castings. The reissues here are the No 23e 'Speed of the Wind' Racing Car and the 23s Streamlined Racing Car. The new castings were the 23f Alfa-Romeo, the 23g Cooper-Bristol, the 23h Ferrari, the 23j HWM, the 23n Maserati and the 23k Talbot-Lago.

The two reissues were interesting, as Meccano described them both as being racing cars when in reality they were not. The Speed of the Wind was built for long-duration land-speed

Emergency vehicles were always popular. The Army version of the Daimler Ambulance was an export-only item and sold in America. In real life, this vehicle was never used by the military as an ambulance.

records and driven by George Eyston. The Streamlined Racing Car was also a land-speed-record car and driven by either George Eyston or John Cobb.

The new castings represented a golden age of motor racing in the 1950s but also a very dangerous time for drivers. Acquiring mint versions of these cars is very difficult, as nearly all the drivers' helmets have lost paint due to accidents while being raced across school yards; current F1 drivers sit very deep in their cars but in the 1950s they were sitting much more upright in the car.

Catalogued by Meccano as racing cars, six of these are from the classic 23 series. The silver-painted 'Speed of the Wind' and the green 'Thunderbolt' were actually land-speed record-breaking cars.

Buses were popular items in toy shops in the 1950s, as car ownership was nothing like today and Dinky always had a good range. The 29 series was also a mixture of reissues and new castings. The reissues were the 29b Streamlined Bus and the 29c Double Deck Bus. The new castings were the 29e Single Deck Bus, the 29f Observation Coach and the 29h Duple Roadmaster Coach.

The streamlined bus was an interesting choice of model by Meccano; it is based on an Albion chassis with a Holland Coachcraft body, which was a very rare vehicle in the UK. There were two versions of the Double Deck Bus, featuring either AEC or Leyland chassis. A useful feature of the Double Deck Bus is that it is built to the same scale as OO model railways and becomes a very useable accessory on layouts. The Luxury Coach and the Observation Coach were on Maudslay chassis and the Single Deck Bus was a generic model, possibly based on a Guy or a Leyland chassis.

This period of Dinky Toy production was very much biased towards the manufacture of diecast toys based on commercial vehicles, and there were numerous new castings. The 511 Guy 4-ton Lorry had been in the range for some time when it was joined by the 551 Large Trailer, the 591 AEC 'Shell' Tanker, the 522 Big Bedford Lorry, the 533 Leyland Comet Cement Wagon and the 581 Horse Box 'British Railways'.

The Horse Box was on a Maudslay chassis and, due to its large physical size, was cast in aluminium and not mazac. The horse alongside the box is from the No. 2 Dinky Farmyard Animals Gift Set and the sacks on the cement truck are Meccano items. Two versions of the AEC Tanker are available, one marked 'Shell Chemicals Limited' and one marked just 'Shell Chemicals'.

Delivery Vans, also known as 'vans with advertising', always figured very strongly in the pre-war Dinky Toys range. This tradition was maintained after the war, and shown here are 14c Coventry Climax Fork Lift Truck, 514 Guy Van 'Slumberland', 31a Trojan 15-cwt Van 'ESSO', the 31d Trojan Van 'OXO', the 30pb Petrol Tanker 'ESSO' and the 30w Electric Articulated Lorry 'British Railways'.

The petrol tanker was based on the Studebaker 2R chassis, while the electric lorry is based on the Jen-Helecs Battery Electric Articulated Vehicle, which was distributed by Hindle Smart & Co. Ltd of Manchester.

Classic Dinky buses of the 1950s. The grey streamlined bus based on the Holland Coachcraft vehicle was fictitious. This vehicle was only made as a van in real life.

Large commercial vehicles. The Shell tanker is on an AEC Monarch chassis. Unlike the Guy and Big Bedford models, this was the only version Dinky made of this vehicle.

The two Guy vans and the two Trojan vans were a foretaste of what was to come over the next few years.

During this period, there were three superb cranes introduced by Meccano. The 752 Goods Yard Crane is loading the 521 Bedford Articulated Lorry with two Hornby O gauge Cable Drums. The 571 Coles Mobile Crane is loading the 30r Fordson 'Thames' Flat Truck with a Hornby Dublo OO gauge Furniture Container, while the 972 Coles 20-ton Lorry Mounted Crane is carrying a Meccano strip.

The Lorry Mounted Crane is a Coles Ranger on an AEC chassis. The Yard Crane was advertised by Meccano in both the Dinky Toys and the Hornby Trains catalogue, as it is

Vans displaying advertising were always popular. This image shows a large disparity in scales; this aspect of modelling never concerned Meccano when making Dinky Toys.

suitable for use with either range of models. Some of the goods yard cranes were made with a cast-iron base.

America was a very big export market for all Meccano products and the distributor for the US was H. Hudson Dobson, which was based in New Jersey. I used to love the American cars; they were very popular here and in the United States.

The 582 Pullmore Bedford Car Transporter was a Dinky bestseller with its huge amount of play value, and it is shown in the illustration with the 139a Ford Fordor Sedan, the 139b Hudson Commodore Sedan and the 172 Studebaker Land Cruiser. Like the horsebox, the trailer part of the car transporter is cast in aluminium, while the Bedford cab is mazac.

Left: Three very popular cranes from the Dinky range. The AEC Coles Ranger in the background was a superb model and offered huge amounts of play value.
Below: Some very popular Dinky American cars from the 1950s. It was a struggle getting them onto the Pullmore Car Transporter due to their size.

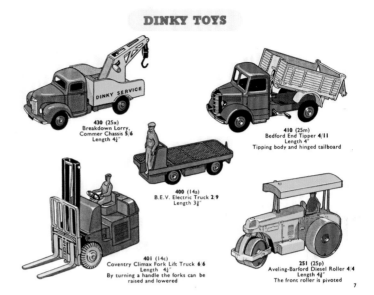

Page 7 from the 1954 Dinky catalogue. This showed both the old reference numbers and the new ones alongside each model. After 1954 only the new numbers were shown.

Some major changes were happening during 1953 and 1954. Up to this point virtually all the toys had been numbered using an alphanumeric system such as 27b or 23e; these were now replaced by numeric catalogue references such as 320 and 221. This meant the end of a system whereby similar groups of toys were catalogued together as a series, i.e., 23 series or 40 series. During 1954 the Dinky catalogue showed the new numbers in bold lettering and the old numbers in brackets; by 1955 only the new numbers were shown.

The other change was to do with boxes, with the trade boxes phased out and the familiar Dinky Yellow individual boxes introduced. As with the catalogues, during the changeover period, the boxes, including trade boxes, showed dual numbers before being changed to show just the new catalogue numbers. The box for the Horse Box shows dual numbers and an LF label; this refers to the use of lead-free paint, which also started to be used at this time.

Examples of packaging, two trade boxes, the very familiar blue-and-white-striped box for the larger models and the yellow box for smaller models. Three different versions of boxes for the Scout car are shown.

5
1954–1959: Consolidation

1954 saw the end of food rationing, which had been in place since 1940. The post-war period of austerity had thankfully come to an end, and the toy shops now had better levels of stock. This was very much a boom period for Meccano, and Dinky Toys in particular were enjoying very good sales, being far and away the market leaders. However, unbeknown to them, serious trouble lay ahead with the launch of Corgi Toys by Mettoy Ltd in 1956. They were very quickly going to become serious competition, not only for Dinky but for many other toy manufacturers.

Surprisingly there were no new Dinky items introduced in either January or February 1954, but March saw the commencement of the superb range of post-war military vehicles, which was, and still is, my favourite Dinky Toys range of all time. Judging from the large amount of mint, and near mint, military toys still available, they were very popular with a lot of boys.

Did you know?

A number of original Meccano factory drawings have survived and these are a valuable information source. An example is drawing number 13,940 for the 621 Three-Ton Army Wagon. The drawing was originated in September 1953 and the model was introduced in May 1954. The following changes are then detailed on the drawing: driver figure added in June 1954, tyres changed from plain to treaded type in April 1958 and cab windows fitted in January 1960. Thus a history can be compiled regarding what changes happened and when.

November 1953 saw the introduction of the 673 Daimler Dingo Scout Car, which was followed in 1954 by the 623 Bedford QL Army Covered Wagon. The real Daimler and the Bedford were well known as they were introduced during the Second World War. The other military vehicles were all post-war and were the 621 Bedford RL 3-ton Army Wagon, 651 Centurion Main Battle Tank, the 622 Foden FG 10-ton Army Truck, the 674 Austin Champ Military Vehicle, the 641 Army 1-ton Humber Cargo Truck and the 670 Daimler Armoured Car.

The surprising choice is the Foden 10-ton army truck, as only two Fodens of this type were ever supplied to the Army – these were trials vehicles for possible use by the Army. The 10-ton vehicle chosen for use by the Armed Forces was the six-wheeled AEC Militant, a very imposing vehicle that Dinky chose not to adopt.

The military range was further enhanced with the introduction of the 692 5.5-inch Medium Gun, the 660 Thornycroft Mighty Antar Tank Transporter (at the time the largest Dinky Supertoy in the range), the 626 Fordson Military Ambulance with opening rear doors, the 677 AEC Armoured Command Vehicle and the 661 Scammell Explorer Recovery Tractor with an operating crane mechanism.

THE MECCANO MAGAZINE

DINKY TOYS

2 **NEW** models ready during March

JAGUAR XK120 COUPE - NO. 157

Prices include Purchase Tax

"Grace... Space... Pace" is a Jaguar slogan and the Jaguar XK120 Coupé possesses these features in good measure. This famous fixed-head two-seater, powered by a 3½-litre 6-cylinder engine, holds numerous world records, and is a leader in its class. Its graceful lines are faithfully reproduced in the Dinky Toys model, which measures 3⅞ inches in length and is available in either bright yellow or bright red.
PRICE 2/8

ARMY COVERED WAGON - NO. 623

A familiar vehicle on British roads is the Army Covered Wagon, on a Bedford 3-ton chassis, and it makes an excellent subject for a fine new Dinky Toy, finished in Service green with the Royal Armoured Corps sign on front and rear. The cover of the wagon is detachable, and the overall length of the miniature is 3½ in. A towing hook is fitted at the rear.
PRICE 3/7

MADE IN ENGLAND BY MECCANO LIMITED

Right: The announcement in the March 1954 Meccano catalogue of the Army Covered Wagon. This was the start of what, over the next ten years, would become a significant range of models.

Below: The first eight models in the post-war military range. The Austin Champ was sold with a driver figure only, while the seated passenger figures shown were available separately.

A number of the military vehicles were enhanced during their lifetime; for example, the 623 Bedford originally had smooth tyres, no driver and no windows. Later versions had treaded tyres, a driver figure and windows added. Similar improvements were added to a lot of the 1950s Dinky Toys.

A good example of the diversity of the military vehicles, including the Thornycroft Mighty Antar Tank Transporter, which was then the largest Dinky Toy in the range.

Did you know?

Gift sets containing Dinky Toys have been an ever present feature of the range. These might have contained a particular type of vehicle such as cars, commercial vehicles, aeroplanes, military vehicles, etc., or a specific theme such as AA or RAC models, building site models, etc. Gift sets continued to be available right up to the closure of the factory. Some of these are highly collectable today.

The last military introductions in the 1950s were the 642 Leyland Hippo RAF Pressure Refueller (this was the only RAF vehicle ever produced by Dinky), the 697 25-pounder Field Gun Gift Set, the 689 Leyland Martian Medium Artillery Tractor, the 693 7.2-inch Howitzer and the 643 Austin K9 200 Gallon Army Water Tanker. The 25-pounder vehicle is on a Morris Quad chassis. The three items contained within the gift set were also available separately.

As well as models meant for sale in all countries, Meccano made a few specifically for the American market. The US-only issues were the 25wm Bedford Military Truck, the 30sm Austin Covered Wagon, the 139am US Army Ford Fordor Staff Car and the 669 USA Army Universal Jeep. The figures come from the 150 Royal Armoured Corps Personnel Gift Set and were only available in the US, which is a real shame, as I think they have great play value and would have sold well in all markets.

Delivery vans have always been very popular with both young boys and Meccano as they are colourful and look really attractive on display in a toy shop. The three Austin vans were the 470 'Shell/BP', the 471 'Nestles' and the 472 'Raleigh Cycles'. These vehicles were based on the very popular Austin Devon 10-cwt van. The 465 Morris Commercial Van 'Capstan' was an interesting choice; all cigarette advertising is banned nowadays, but life was very

The Leyland Pressure Refueller was the only RAF vehicle ever made by Dinky. This group includes four vehicles sold only in America.

different back in 1957, when smoking was still socially acceptable. This van was based on the Morris Commercial J-type 10-cwt van.

There were four more Trojan 15-cwt vans in this period and these were the 451 'Dunlop', the 452 'Chivers', the 454 'Cydrax' and the 455 'Brooke Bond Tea'. The Brooke Bond van was the sixth in this series of vans and this specific version is a promotional issue and very rare. There is a label on the roof of the van and on the box stating: 'Since 1924 more than 5,700 Trojan "Little Red Vans" supplied. Replaced on a long-life basis'. It is believed that this

Three delightful Austin Devon delivery vans and, a very strange choice, the Morris J van in 'Capstan' Cigarettes livery – this would certainly not be allowed today.

promotional vehicle was commissioned by Trojan Ltd. It is not known whether Trojan or Meccano applied the labels.

The Bedford CA Van with its sliding front doors was a very popular vehicle in the 1950s, and the Dinky version is the original type with split front windows. The three variants are the 480 Bedford 10-cwt Van 'Kodak', the 481 Bedford 10-cwt Van 'Ovaltine' and the 482 Bedford 10-cwt Van 'Dinky Toys'. The 480 Bedford Kodak van is the last small vehicle to have been supplied in a trade box of six, except for the 687 25-pounder trailer, which, on its own, was only ever supplied in trade boxes.

Recently thirty-three printers' Dinky box proofs were found in an attic of a house in Manchester. The house had previously been owned by a commercial artist called Herbert Roddis, who died in 1979. Since this discovery I have contacted nearly twenty museums, art galleries and newspapers in the Manchester area in the hope of discovering any information about Mr Roddis; unfortunately, this has all been to no avail.

There were lots of other box proofs for cosmetic products, soaps, seeds, etc., and they probably formed part of his portfolio, or were possibly items he kept for personal reasons. As Manchester is not far from Liverpool, it is reasonable to assume that he either worked for Meccano, or was a sub-contractor. This discovery is proof that there is potentially still lots to find hidden away in attics and cellars.

Left: A very familiar sight on the streets of Britain in the 1950s was the Trojan van. Four Dinky versions are shown; the 'Brooke Bond Tea' special promotional one is rare.

Below: Also a familiar van was the Bedford CA. Dinky modelled the early version with the split windscreen.

The proof shown is of the 283 BOAC Coach, which was introduced in 1956. It is on a Commer chassis with a Harrington Contender thirty-five-seat body.

Dinky added further to the racing and sports car range with the 237 Mercedes-Benz Racing Car, the 163 Bristol 450 Sports Coupe, the 236 Connaught Racing Car, the 107 Sunbeam Alpine Sports Car and the 239 Vanwall Racing Car.

The Bristol 450 is an interesting choice for Dinky, as only four were ever built and were successful at Le Mans in 1954 and 1955. After the disaster in 1955, Bristol withdrew from racing and destroyed three of the cars. The Mercedes was based on the streamlined version of the W196 model. At the end of 1955 they also withdrew from racing until their return as a constructor in 2009.

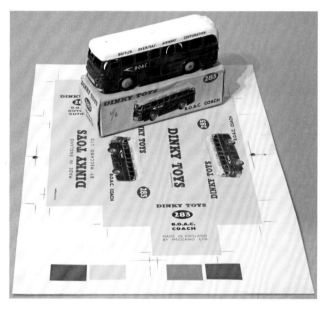

Right: The BOAC Coach and its box, plus a printer's proof of the same box, which was a recent 'attic find'. Who knows what is still out there, lying undiscovered?
Below: Five sports and grand prix racing cars. The Bristol 450 Coupe (number 27) deserves a mention; only four of these cars were ever built and they won their class at Le Mans in 1953 and 1954.

Some iconic racing cars of the 1950s. It was normal for Dinky to supply cars already carrying racing numbers. The D-Type Jaguar was the exception, and it came plain, with a packet containing three sets of racing numbers sold separately.

Four very popular sports cars were the 133 Cunningham C-5R Road Racer, the 110 Aston Martin DB3 Sports Car, the 108 MG Midget Sports Car and the iconic 238 Jaguar Type D Racing Car. The Cunningham C-5R Racer was also an interesting choice, as it was only raced for one season, with the highlight being third place in the 1953 Le Mans 24 Hours race.

Surprisingly the Jaguar was issued in Turquoise rather than the much more usual British Racing Green, and this was the only racing car issued by Dinky without a racing number. The *Meccano Magazine* of September 1957 stated, '"A packet containing three sets of racing numbers is available for use with this and other appropriate racing cars." Price 3d. (inc. Tax)'

In the *Meccano Magazine* of May 1959, there are construction details, photographs and a list of parts required to build a working Dinky Toys display. This is of a similar design to one they supplied to dealers but it is safe as it does not have a mains-driven motor. I decided to make one of these as a winter project and mechanically to reproduce it as closely as possible to the original concept. It uses a Meccano E020 20-V motor and is run from a Meccano T20 Transformer, which has an adjustable output. I have found that the ideal performance is achieved with the motor running on the lowest voltage setting from the transformer.

The vehicles are moved by an endless belt running around four pulleys. Four steel pins are securely fixed to this belt, and they engage with a small hole drilled into the baseplate of each of the models. I extended the depth of the roadbed by approximately 100 mm at the rear to allow room for some low relief buildings, which enabled me to create a small diorama to produce an interesting display.

The Dinky Toys on here are the 109 Austin Healey 100 Sports Car, the 157 Jaguar XK120 Sports Coupe, the 641 Army 1-ton Cargo Truck, the 261 Telephone Service Van, the 3f Woman, the 3d Female Hiker, the 750 Telephone Box, the 760 Pillar Box, three road signs from the 47 Gift Set, the 6a Shepherd, the 6b Sheep-dog and twelve 2d Sheep.

I have shown this in various places and it always attracts much interest. I would thoroughly recommend this as an interesting project and a very satisfying challenge.

The working Dinky Toys display is a recreation of an item featured in the May 1959 *Meccano Magazine*. It has drawn huge interest wherever it has been shown and was a fascinating project.

The Post Office services vehicles and accessories are very colourful and attractive models. The three vehicles were the 34b Morris Commercial Royal Mail Van, the 260 Morris J Royal Mail Van and the 261 Morris Z Telephone Service Van. The other items were the 750 Telephone Box, the 760 Pillar Box, the 12d Telegraph Messenger and the 12e Postman.

Morris vehicles were obviously very popular with the Post Office. There was a 299 Post Office Services Gift Set issued in 1957, which surprisingly omitted the Pillar Box.

Meccano obviously concentrated the majority of their production on British vehicles but they did also make some very nice foreign vehicle models, such as the 181 Volkswagen Saloon. Shown here are some of the last models to be produced without windows, including the 157 Jaguar XK120 Coupe, the 162 Ford Zephyr Saloon, the 164 Vauxhall Cresta Saloon, the 156 Rover 75 Saloon and the 190 Touring Caravan.

Nabisco Foods of Welwyn Garden City used to produce Shredded Wheat and they had a promotional special offer regarding Dinky Toys. If you sent in twelve Shredded Wheat box tops you could receive a free toy car, the Volkswagen being one of them. Also available as part of this offer were the 155 Ford Anglia and the 167 AC Aceca – there may have been others.

Before privatisation these were all known as GPO products and were very popular. The Royal Mail van with the GR crest was initially a pre-war issue and was reissued afterwards. It is now highly collectable.

The 176 Austin A105 Saloon was launched in April 1958 and was available in two colour schemes: a Cream body with a Blue side flash or a Pale Grey body with a Red side flash. Other colour schemes were to follow later. It was an excellent representation of a luxury Austin saloon.

Mettoy launched Corgi Toys in 1956; from the outset they were called 'The Ones With Windows', a feature that Dinky had only included in open-topped sports cars. I suspect that

A selection of 1950s cars and a caravan. These were among the last Dinky Toys cars to be issued without windows. The Volkswagen with white tyres was part of a promotion with Nabisco Foods Ltd, who were the owners of Shredded Wheat.

Meccano were starting to see their sales decline, and the subsequent Austin A105 was the first Dinky Toy with windows. The battle of the features had begun and, for the foreseeable future, the two companies desperately tried to outdo each other.

From this point onwards all Dinky Toys cars were fitted with windows, and further features started to arrive. Here we have the 166 Sunbeam Rapier Saloon, the 167 AC Aceca Coupe, the 168 Singer Gazelle Saloon, the 150 Rolls-Royce Silver Wraith, the 189 Triumph Herald Saloon, the 165 Humber Hawk Saloon and the 187 Volkswagen Karmann Ghia Coupe.

The Rolls-Royce was the first Dinky Toys car to be fitted with independent spring suspension, and the Triumph Herald, the Humber Hawk and the Volkswagen Karmann Ghia were also fitted with this system. I have a 1958 Dinky Toys leaflet that makes reference to 'Glydwell Independent Suspension', but I have never seen the term 'Glydwell' on any other Dinky literature. I wonder if the term had already been patented by another company and they had to stop using it.

Following the tradition of admirable American cars, Dinky made four very colourful models, the 132 Packard Convertible, the 131 Cadillac Eldorado Tourer, the 173 Nash Rambler and the 174 Hudson Hornet Sedan. These models were fine examples, and the only thing

Right: April 1958 was an important month for Dinky Toys. The *Meccano Magazine* proudly announced the Austin A105 Saloon Car 'with windows'. They had been forced to follow the trend started earlier by Corgi Toys and, thus, a race to be the first with innovative features on toys had begun.
Below: Some of the first Dinky Toys cars fitted with windows. The Rolls-Royce was another first for Dinky as it was fitted with independent suspension. As can be seen, this was a large model to represent an equally large real-life car.

I have a doubt about is the size of the drivers in the Packard and the Cadillac. They look somewhat oversized as they are both looking over the top of the windscreen.

The breadth of the aircraft range after the war was never as great as that from before, but the quality of what was offered was every bit as good. Here we have the ill-fated 702 DH Comet Airliner, the 736 Hawker Hunter Fighter, the 734 Vickers Supermarine Swift Fighter and the 735 Gloster Javelin Delta Wing Fighter. The age of the jet had well and truly arrived in the Dinky catalogue.

The 702 was based on the de Havilland DH-106 Comet 1, which was the first passenger jet aircraft in the world. Sadly there were a number of severe problems with the Comet 1 and they were all withdrawn from service. The Comet was eventually very successful but only after the fuselage had been substantially redesigned.

Four lovely American automobiles from Packard, Cadillac, Hudson and Nash. Similarly to the British car industry, three of these famous names have now disappeared and only Cadillac survives.

The post-war Dinky aircraft range was much smaller but the quality did not diminish. These are three lovely small military planes from Gloster, Supermarine and Hawker. The ill-fated DH Comet airliner did eventually become successful after the fuselage was redesigned.

The final iteration of the Fodens arrived in June 1955 with the superb 942 'Regent Tanker'. This was followed by the first two models of the new Dinky eight-wheeled truck, which were the 934 Leyland Octopus Wagon and the 943 Leyland Octopus Tanker 'ESSO'.

Did you know?

The colour scheme of some models were only in the range for a short period of time. This can have a huge effect on the value of certain items. An example is the 934 Leyland Octopus Wagon, shown here in green and yellow; this is the common version. If this model were in dark blue and pale yellow, it could be valued at up to £3,500.

The Leyland Octopus was truly a worthy successor to the Fodens as it captured the real-world vehicle very faithfully. This would have been a very cost-effective production for Meccano as the bodies were the same as those used to very great effect on the Foden trucks.

With Meccano being based in Liverpool, I suspect someone saw a propeller on a low loader and it inspired the 986 civilian version of the Thornycroft Mighty Antar with the propeller load. It used the same prime mover as the 660 Tank Transporter but with a different semi-trailer designed to carry the impressive propeller load. It could well have been escorted by the 255 Mersey Tunnel Police Van, which was based on a Land Rover chassis.

Another vehicle with huge play value was the 965 Euclid Rear Dump Truck – I know mine moved huge amounts of earth. The 765 Road Hoarding was a useful accessory with Dinky Toys and Hornby Trains, but sadly the posters have now discoloured due to a reaction to the adhesive on the back of the posters over a number of years.

The December 1955 *Meccano Magazine* showed two splendid new large delivery vans on the rear cover: the 923 Big Bedford Van 'Heinz' and the 918 Guy Van 'Ever Ready'. Eighteen months later the final Guy van arrived – the 919 Robertson's 'Golden Shred' version.

The last iteration of the much-loved Foden in stunning 'Regent' colours and the replacement eight wheeler, the Leyland Octopus. All these vehicles were absolute showstoppers in the toy shops, and are still much admired today.

Two impressive, large commercials and the iconic Mersey Tunnel Police Van. They are in front of the road hoarding from 1959, featuring the famous English cricketer Denis Compton, who was also an FA Cup winner with Arsenal.

The Guy vans had six completely different liveries throughout their lifetime, whereas the Big Bedford only featured Heinz, albeit one had a baked beans can and the other had a '57 Varieties' ketchup bottle. The ketchup bottle version is much rarer and more difficult to find.

In 1959 Dinky released three superb, and completely different, commercial vehicles. They were the 968 BBC TV Karrier Roving Eye Vehicle, the 967 BBC TV Morris Commercial Mobile

The last two versions of the Guy Vixen delivery vans, including the 'Golden Shred' version featuring the now politically incorrect golliwog. Unlike the Guy vans, Dinky only ever did the Big Bedford van in a 'Heinz' livery, albeit with two variants.

Control Room and the 969 BBC TV Bedford Extending Mast Vehicle. All the vehicles were in the BBC corporate dark green colour. Nowadays with our skies absolutely full of satellites we take outside broadcasting for granted and the whole process can be done from a small van. In 1969 this was totally new technology and it need three large vehicles to perform this function. Dinky followed these later with a couple of similar vehicles for the independent broadcaster ABC-TV.

The dealer support from Meccano was always very comprehensive. As well as the dealer flier shown earlier, boxes of 200 price tickets were available; these were updated as the range changed or the prices were amended. The freestanding card 'Dinky Toys for Variety and Value' was one of a number of similar items promoting the range. These were printed in many different languages for use by dealers overseas. In addition, illuminated signs, glass-fronted display cabinets, revolving metal point-of-sale displays and many other items could be supplied to dealers.

Right: The race is now underway, with the BBC providing live coverage via the outside broadcasting vehicles. I suspect that the Mercedes-Benz just disappearing round the corner will win this race.

Below: Meccano were excellent at producing point-of-sale material and here we see Dinky price tickets, a Dinky Toys paperweight and a cardboard label that was available in different languages.

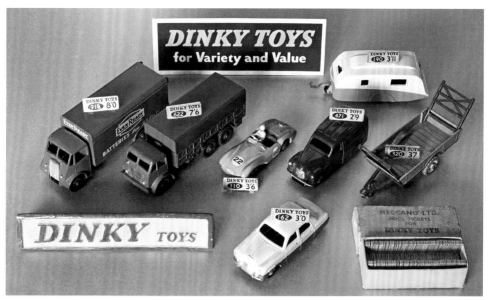

6
1960–1969: Features Galore

Meccano was starting to feel pressure from all sides during the 1960s. The Hornby 'O' trains were being discontinued, primarily because houses were becoming smaller. The quality of Hornby Dublo was unquestioned but they were very expensive when compared to Tri-ang and other OO gauge products. Furthermore, Lego was now proving to be a serious competitor to Meccano. Adding further problems to all of this was the fact that the toy market in the UK was in decline.

The race between Dinky Toys and Corgi Toys to be the first to the market with new features was now incredibly intense and every few months something new was being announced by one company or the other.

Three vehicles brimming with features were added to the military range; these were the 666 Corporal Missile Erector Vehicle with Corporal Missile and Launching Vehicle, the 667 Corporal Missile Servicing Platform Vehicle and the 665 Honest John Missile Launcher. Both these missiles were capable of being fired via a spring-loaded mechanism and were full of excellent play value.

The Corporal erector vehicle was based on a LeTourneau chassis and British firing took place on the Scottish Outer Hebrides. The servicing platform and the Honest John launcher were based on an International chassis, and the Honest John was fired by the Royal Artillery on the Hohne Ranges in North Germany.

Dinky had now entered the rocket age with the Corporal and Honest John missile systems. Both were capable of carrying a nuclear weapon but thankfully the Dinky versions were not. The miniature versions could be fired in a realistic fashion.

Did you know?

In order to circumvent importing restrictions during the 1960s, raw castings of approximately twenty cars were sent to the Meccano agent Arthur E. Harris (Pty) Ltd in South Africa. These were then painted and assembled locally, and packaged in boxes printed in English and Afrikaans. I have a display card showing 'De allernieuwste' Dinky Toys, which means 'The best choice' in Afrikaans; this was probably made for A. E. Harris.

Dinky Toys sprung a surprise in February 1960 with the announcement of the 785 Service Station Kit. This was a plastic self-assembly kit and had beige walls, a red roof and grey floor. Construction was quite straightforward, with clear instructions supplied. Introduced at the same time was the battery-operated 787 Lighting Kit, suitable for use with this and other buildings.

As can be seen, the 781 Petrol Pump Station 'ESSO' and figures from the 009 Service Station Personnel Set made the basis for an excellent play scene. The maker of the yellow car ramp is not known, as Dinky never made one of these. The Paintwork & Bodywork building is handmade from card and my inspiration for this was 'The Toyman', who promoted new Dinky models each month in the *Meccano Magazine*.

The second self-assembly building was the 954 Fire Station Kit. This was another very well-designed kit and is quite rare nowadays. The 787 Lighting Kit is ideal for this building, as is the 009 Fire Station Personnel Set. Also shown are the 257 Nash Rambler Canadian 'Fire Chief' Car, the 555 Fire Engine, the 956 Turntable Fire Escape Lorry, the 250 Streamlined Fire Engine, the 490 Electric Dairy Van 'Express Dairy', the 280 Delivery Van, the 470 Austin A40 Van 'Shell-BP', the 254 Austin Taxi and the 269 Jaguar Motorway Police Car.

The inspiration for the delivery van is not known; a Bedford van has been suggested as the prototype but it probably is just a generic vehicle. The diesel tank at the rear is all that remains of my old Foden tanker of the 1950s.

The 292 Leyland Atlantean Bus is the 'Ribble' version. There was another livery marked 'Corporation Transport', also, and both of these are to be found with a plain

A busy scene at the Dinky Service Station. This self-assembly kit was very realistic and a popular item at the time.

The Dinky fire brigade has been called out on an emergency and the policeman is controlling the traffic. This was also a self-assembly kit like the service station.

Four public transport vehicles. The 'Exide' bus and the Leyland Atlantean were suitable for use with 00 gauge model railway systems. The Atlas Kenebrake bus featured an independent suspension system.

upper panel or with advertising for 'Regent' petrol. The 291 London Bus 'Exide Batteries' was the last version of the long running 29c/290 bus casting. This was the first time that the colour scheme was totally red and Dinky had called it a London bus. This was the Leyland chassis version. The 283 'BOAC' Coach was based on Commer running gear with a Harrington body. The 295 Standard Atlas Kenebrake Minibus was introduced in May 1960. This was the first Dinky bus with windows and interior seating. It also featured spring suspension.

One of the most recognisable images of London must be the iconic Routemaster Bus. Dinky Toys did not disappoint with their superb rendition of this vehicle as catalogue number 289, first introduced in 1964. The model has windows, a driver figure, and a conductress on the rear platform. Four liveries are shown: 'Tern' Shirts; 'ESSO Safety Grip' tyres; and two different 'Madame Tussaud's' adverts. All five buses were on Route 221 to King's Cross. The Routemaster bus was on an AEC chassis.

In the early 1970s high-quality commercials were still being produced. The Coles Crane and the Johnston Road Sweeper are examples of model making at its very best.

Truck features raising and lowering fork blades, driver, detailed engine and a pallet. The 430 Johnson 2 Ton Dumper has steering, tipping bucket and a driver figure.

The convoy series of vehicles was not for the traditional Dinky Toy collector but firmly intended for much younger customers. They all had a generic cab with windows and cab interior, and all shared the same chassis. Only the bodies, and colour schemes provided variations to the models. This would have made this a very cost-effective range of trucks. Despite all this, the models do have a certain charm. The vehicle types were the 380 Skip Truck, the 381 Farm Truck, the 382 Dumper Truck, the 383 'National Carriers' truck, the 384 Fire Rescue Truck, the 385 'Royal Mail' Truck and the 687 Army Truck.

Nice police cars were produced right up to the end, and here we have the 277 Police Land Rover, which features an opening bonnet and engine, a blue roof light and a policeman; the 243 Volvo Police Car with opening rear tailgate, four traffic cones, a police slow sign, a police dog and a policeman; the 269 Ford Transit Police Accident Unit with opening door and tailgate, police signs, four cones, roof light and a policeman; and the 254 Police Range Rover with opening doors, tailgate, bonnet, engine detail and a roof light. Lastly, on secondment from America, we have the 244 Plymouth Gran Fury Police Car with roof light bar, siren and radio aerial.

The last emergency vehicles were of mixed quality. The 282 Land Rover Fire Appliance has opening doors and bonnet with engine detail, removable ladder, spotlight and hoses. The 263 ERF Airport Fire Rescue Tender has a removable ladder and roof detail, while the 266 ERF Fire Tender is the same casting as the 263 but with a removable escape ladder – clever utilisation of resources by Meccano. The 276 Ford Transit Ambulance has an opening door and rear tailgate, a patient on a stretcher and a roof light. Next are two more American

The range of Convoy vehicles was another attempt to save money. All were made on a generic chassis with different types of bodies; a lot of plastic was used in these vehicles.

A nice selection of police vehicles. Many of these items came with figures, signs and traffic cones to allow a realistic scene to be set up.

Some nice emergency vehicles. The Airport Rescue and the Fire Tender were both on the same AEC casting but with different ladders. The ambulances came with a patient on a stretcher.

vehicles: the 288 Superior Cadillac Ambulance has an opening tailgate with a patient on a stretcher. The 267 Dodge Paramedic Truck was from the television series *Emergency* and comes with two paramedics and an 'Emergency Squad' badge.

Two small 410 Bedford CF delivery vans are next, one in 'Royal Mail' and the other in 'AA Service' liveries. The Bedford CF was available in many different colour schemes, and two of them are shown here. The 604 Land Rover Bomb Disposal Unit is the same casting as the 254 Police vehicle. A Remote Controlled Vehicle (RCV), known as a 'Wheelbarrow', is included with this model.

A Land Rover and two Bedford CF vans. The Land Rover is a military bomb-disposal vehicle and comes with an assembly kit to make a 'wheelbarrow' remote-controlled vehicle.

British, European and American cars still dominated the range. Japanese cars had just started to arrive and this corresponded with the demise of Meccano; consequently no Far Eastern cars were ever in the Dinky catalogue. Here we have the 115 Plymouth Fury Open Sports with opening bonnet, engine detail, twin aerials, driver, passenger, suspension and steering. The 192 Range Rover featured opening bonnet, doors and tailgate, tipping seats and engine detail, while the 124 Rolls-Royce Phantom V Saloon had opening doors, boot, chauffeur and suspension. The 128 Mercedes-Benz 600 saloon was the same casting as the red one shown earlier, but it had now lost the chauffeur and passengers. The Mercedes-Benz C111 was based on a concept car and had opening gull wing doors, opening rear boot, engine detail and suspension. The 123 Austin Princess 2200HL saloon only had windows and an interior. As can be seen, the detailing and features were disappearing.

Three attractive taxis start with the 284 London Taxi, colloquially known as the 'Black Cab'. It was based on the Austin FX4, and had opening doors, suspension and a driver figure. The 241 Silver Jubilee Taxi was of the same casting but was released to celebrate the Silver Jubilee of Her Majesty the Queen in 1977. The 278 Plymouth Gran Fury Yellow Cab features a sign on the cab roof and an aerial.

The first Dinky Toys Action Kits were introduced in 1971. There were thirty-four kits issued in total and they covered models of cars, commercials, public transport, military and aeroplanes. The model shown is catalogue number 1017 and it is the 289 Routemaster London Bus. It included paint, instructions and assembly screws.

In 1979 Meccano introduced two Dinky Builda kits made from self-coloured cardboard; these were Blazing Inferno and Space-War Station. The kits incorporate pre-glued tabs, and the parts just press out of the two sheets in the kit. While the kits are fiddly, they are relatively straightforward to assemble. Shown is the assembled Blazing Inferno scene along with the 250 Streamlined Fire Engine, the 955 Commer Fire Engine, the 956 Bedford Turntable Fire Escape Lorry and figures from the 008 Fire Station Personnel Gift Set.

In 1973 Meccano experimented with making a model to a larger than normal scale of 1:25. They were all variants of a Ford Capri 3 Litre, with a standard saloon, a police car and a rally car. These were not successful and were discontinued in 1976, making them now quite rare.

Some of the last cars from Dinky. In another cost-saving exercise the Austin Princess had virtually no features and feels very flimsy.

Above: Two versions of the Austin FX4 London Taxi and a Plymouth Yellow Cab with a rather over-sized aerial. The black cab and the yellow cab were both very iconic vehicles.

Right: A Dinky Action Kit of the London Routemaster Bus from 1971. This came complete with instructions, paint, transfers and screws for assembly. Meccano was owned at this time by Airfix and the concept of self-assembly kits would have come from them.

The Dinky Builda Blazing Inferno cardboard assembly kit. It was a little bit fiddly to build, but huge play value when completed.

Shown is the 2253 Police Car version: the large size can be seen alongside the 269 Jaguar Police Car. The Capri features windows, detailed interior, tipping seat backs, opening boot, opening bonnet with very detailed engine, wing mirror, windscreen wipers, roof-mounted sign and blue light, warning light on boot lid, twin exhausts and detailed head and tail lights. This size of vehicle was not repeated by Meccano.

In 1974 Dinky made three large models of the Ford Capri to a scale of 1:24. The police version is shown here, alongside the Jaguar police car. This large scale was a short-lived experiment.

From the 1970s there were television-related items such as the 602 Armoured Command Car, which was designed by Gerry Anderson for the proposed television series *The Investigator* that only ever had a pilot episode. The 361 Zygon Galactic War Chariot was issued in 1979, and has two figures and fires missiles.

During the last couple of years of Meccano, the Dinky 'Customised' range was launched. These items were existing castings revisited with various embellishments. The 202 Land Rover was the 344 casting; the 203 Range Rover was the 192 casting; the 206 Corvette Stingray was the 221 casting; and the 390 Freeway Cruiser was the third casting of the Transit Van 269. All have wide wheels, large exhausts on the side and other added features.

Two science fiction vehicles from the late 1970s, depicting an Armoured Command Vehicle (ACV) designed by Gerry Anderson and a rocket-firing Zygon Patroller.

The standard model of the 362 Trident Starfighter was introduced in 1979 and finished in black. It was capable of firing missiles. Shown is the special edition painted in gold, which has a label containing the following text: 'This Dinky Toy model has been produced specially to commemorate the Airfix Group Dinner Dance at the London Hilton, on 18 September 1979'. I believe the signature is by Ray McNeice, who was the last Managing Director of Meccano.

Twelve days after being presented with this gift, all the recipients were made redundant.

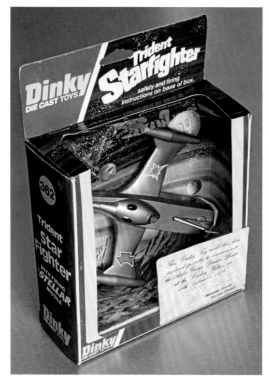

Above: Four customised vehicles, which bore little relation to reality. These are good examples of the parlous state of the Dinky designs just before the demise of the company.
Left: Probably the most poignant image in the book: twelve days after presenting these as gifts at a dinner the Meccano factory was closed down.

9
What Now?

Collecting Dinky Toys

There are many ways to acquire Dinky Toys. In the early days of collecting, the traditional route used to be auction houses, and these are still very active today. Some of them specialise in toy auctions as their prime business. A large number of other auction houses hold specialist toy auctions on a regular basis. The leading auction houses are Vectis Auctions of Stockton-on-Tees, Collectoys of Bourges in France, SAS of Newbury in Berkshire, Astons in the West Midlands, Lacy Scott and Knight of Bury St Edmunds, and Sheffield Auction Gallery. With all of these establishments customers can either place bids live on the internet, lodge an absentee bid or attend the auction and bid on the day. In addition there are many internet auction sites.

Toy fairs are another excellent way to buy, one of the advantages being that you can actually see the item and negotiate a price. These are held virtually every weekend of the year up and down the UK, with the major fairs organised by BP Fairs, J&J Fairs Ltd, SRP Toyfairs, Bulldog Fairs, Tony Oakes Fairs and many others.

Specialist magazines are an excellent source of information, with *Model Collector*, *Diecast Collector* and *Collectors Gazette* all published monthly. As well as containing detailed articles written by specialists, they contain a list of dates for the various auctions and toy fairs. They are available via subscription or from newsagents.

The Dinky Toys Collectors' Association (DTCA) is a membership club specialising in Dinky Toys that publishes a quarterly gazette. It also has a very informative website and an active members' forum.

There is also an absolute wealth of information on the internet covering Meccano, Dinky Toys, Dinky Builder, Hornby Trains, Hornby Dublo and Bayko.

Museums

Brighton Toy and Model Museum, Trafalgar Street, Brighton, BN1 4EB
The Cotswold Motoring Museum & Toy Collection, Sherbourne Street, Bourton-on-the Water, GL54 2BY
South Yorkshire Transport Museum, Waddington Way, Aldwarke, Rotherham, S65 3SH
Tintagel Toy Museum, Fore Street, Tintagel, PL34 0DD
V&A Museum of Childhood, Cambridge Heath Road, London, E2 9PA. (A small collection)

It is advisable to check opening times before travelling to any museum.

Publications

There have been many books on Meccano and Dinky Toys and the following titles are recommended reading:
Brown, Kenneth, *Factory of Dreams, A History of Meccano Ltd* (Crucible Books Ltd: Lancaster, 2007). *An in-depth investigation into the Binns Road factory.*

Busfield, David, *Dinky Toys: A Pictorial Record* (David Busfield: 2013). *The first coverage of 1950s and '60s Dinky Toys using large full colour illustrations.*

Gibson, Cecil, *History of British Dinky Toys 1934–1964* (Model Aeronautical Press Ltd: 1966). *The first serious book covering Dinky Toys.*

McReavy, Anthony, *The Toy Story: The Life and Times of Inventor Frank Hornby* (Ebury Press: London, 2002). *An in-depth study of Frank Hornby, the inventor and the businessman.*

Richardson, Mike and Sue, *Dinky Toys and Modelled Miniatures* (New Cavendish Books: London, 1981). *A major reference work that every collector should own.*

Richardson, Mike and Sue, *The Great Book Of Dinky Toys* (New Cavendish Books: London, 2000). *A superb follow-up to their first book giving more detailed model information, factory drawings, etc.*

Wyborn, Ronald, *Binns Road: An Empire Fallen* (Hornby Railway Collectors' Association: 2010). *This is a must-read booklet by an author who was the head of design and research at Meccano for many years.*